JOBS IN MEDIA

PETER TURNER

WORKING IN AUSTRALIA

REDBACK publishing

First published 2022 by
Redback Publishing
Australia

www.redbackpublishing.com.au
orders@redbackpublishing.com.au

ISBN 978-1-761400-33-9 PBK

Author: Peter Turner
Editor: Caroline Thomas
Designer: Redback Publishing

Original illustrations © Redback Publishing 2024
Originated by Redback Publishing

NATIONAL LIBRARY OF AUSTRALIA
A catalogue record for this book is available from the National Library of Australia

Acknowledgements
Abbreviations: l—left, r—right, b—bottom, t—top, c—centre, m—middle
We would like to thank the following for permission to reproduce photographs: (Images © shutterstock)

p5br Moscow, Russia - Aug 30, 2016: Girl (with model release) scroll text on interactive screen in history park Russia - My History in VDNKh. Museum presents key points of development of Russian state. By Pavel L Photo and Video, via Shutterstock.com,
p13b Kuala Lumpur, Malaysia - Dec 3: An unidentified artist showcases a digital sketching of a concept car during Kuala Lumpur International Motor Show on December 8, 2010 in Kuala Lumpur Malaysia. By pistolseven, via Shutterstock.com,
p14t Dnepropetrovsk, Ukraine - Dec.17: "Four seasons" Chamber Orchestra - main conductor Druzelub Yanakiev perform music of Mozart, Elgar, Brittain, Dvorak on Dec. 17, 2012 in Dnepropetrovsk, Ukraine. By Igor Bulgarin, via Shutterstock.com,
p16t Milovice, Czech Republic - October 23, 2013: Filming of the new movie The Knights directed by Carsten Gutschmidt near Milovice, Czech Republic, by Vladimir Wrangel, via Shutterstock.com,
p20br Bangkok, Thailand - Apr 26, 2018: Avenger Infinity War Movie promotional event and toy sale exhibition booth held in shopping center in Bangkok, Thailand, by Sushiman, via Shutterstock.com,
p22t Moscow, Russia - Aug 30, 2016: Girl and boy (with model releases) stand near screen in history park Russia - My History at VDNKh. Museum is designed for simultaneous presence up to 5 thousand people, by Pavel L Photo and Video, via Shutterstock.com,
p23b Les Baux de Provence / France - 07 13 2019: people enjoying view on Van Gogh's painting Wheatfield with crows during light and art multimedia show in Carrières de Lumières museum in Provence, Europe. By Kamilalala, via Shutterstock.com,
p26t New York - June 23: Collage of neon lights, street signs and advertisements at Times Square in New York City on June 23, 2013. Times Square holds the annual New Year's Eve ball drop, by Allen.G, via Shutterstock.com,
p31b p4 Milan, Italy - April 15, 2017: Unidentified actors shooting a history film at Piazza del Duomo square in front of Milan Cathedral (Duomo di Milano), by RukiMedia, via Shutterstock.com

CONTENTS

JOBS IN THE MEDIA

Technology has advanced the media industry more in the last 40 years than at any other time throughout history. It is a dynamic and rapidly growing field of study and the job possibilities are vast.

• WORK TYPES

KEY AREAS IN MEDIA

- PRINT AND DIGITAL MEDIA
- FILM AND TELEVISION
- RADIO
- MULTIMEDIA

There are many exciting jobs within each of these different types of media, both in the public eye and behind the scenes.

PRINT AND ONLINE MEDIA

Print media is the oldest form of mass communication in Australia. It includes newspapers and magazines. Online media includes websites, digital magazines, blogs and social media. There are many jobs in both forms of media, and each one calls for a very different set of skills and very different types of personalities.
Some of these jobs include:

- **editor**
- writer
- photographer
- graphic designer
- printer
- distributor
- retailer
- blogger
- content writer

RADIO

There are many radio stations in Australia and a diverse range of content. Features include interviews and discussions on a huge range of topics including current affairs, science, art, books, movies, food and technology. There are high profile on-air roles as well as careers in programming, creative story telling, engineering, promotions and administration, sales and marketing.

FILM AND TELEVISION

Some people become very famous from being on television or in films. They can earn lots of money, have a strong online presence through entertainment websites and can feature in **advertising campaigns** on billboards, magazines and newspapers. However, most of the work involved in making a film or television show is done behind the scenes. Next time you watch a television program or go to a movie, have a look at the credits. You'll see how many people it takes to produce a film or a television program.

MULTIMEDIA

Multimedia is the integration of different kinds of media, such as text, graphics, animation, sound, video and live action performance. Multimedia can be used in museum displays where interactive video games, film and on-demand audio bring displays to life. Used in industry, interactive digital modelling can accompany live presentations and physical structures or prototypes. Multimedia is used in areas such as education, the arts and business.

PRODUCING RADIO

Radio programs offer a mix of local, national and international news, talkback, music programs and general entertainment. Listening to the radio is very popular in Australia and the growth of digital radio has created new opportunities in this field.

RADIO PRODUCER

JOB DESCRIPTION

Radio producers work behind the scenes to put radio programs together. They also manage what's happening in the studio while the show is being broadcast. Radio producers need to be organised and able to work well under pressure. They must be able to respond to anything that might happen unexpectedly in the studio during a **live** broadcast. They also have to be self-motivated and creative.

RANGE OF WORK:

- find interesting stories
- set up interviews
- write scripts
- organise broadcaster's and guest programming
- coordinate music and advertisements
- make sure all the technical aspects are working
- deal with any problems and make decisions

EDUCATION AND TRAINING

Most radio producers have a degree in journalism, a graduate diploma in radio or a diploma in audio engineering and sound production. Experience in research or other forms of media might also be useful. Working skills are often learned on-the-job and the industry sometimes offers **internship** opportunities.

RADIO JOURNALIST

JOB DESCRIPTION

Radio journalists research and put together news stories. Stories may include current events and topics of general interest that are prepared in a way that makes them interesting for radio. Some journalists work on a variety of topics and some specialise in a particular area, such as sport, finance or politics. As radio journalists work in teams, they must enjoy working with other people. They need to be self-motivated, have good research skills and be able to work to a deadline.

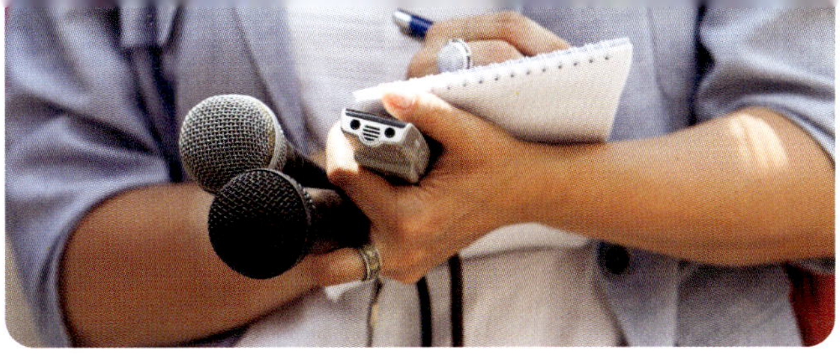

RANGE OF WORK:

- keep up-to-date with news and current affairs
- find news stories from Australia and overseas
- research new news stories
- interview people and record information
- organise information for its best use in radio
- write and present the story

EDUCATION AND TRAINING

There are no specific educational requirements for this job, but a background in journalism would be helpful. People interested in this career should consider completing a degree or a diploma in journalism or broadcasting. Many journalists also have a degree in a particular area of interest, such as science, politics or economics.

TIP

*Get some broad media qualifications and then get experience any way you can, including volunteer or **freelance** work, or apply for an internship.*

'...get experience any way you can ...'

BROADCASTING ON AIR

When we listen to the radio,there are many people besides the presenter who play an important part in what we hear. Sound technicians and engineers are extremely important people in the production of a radio program.

• RADIO SOUND OPERATOR

JOB DESCRIPTION

Some radio programs are pre-recorded. Sound operators are responsible for recording sounds and audio and making sure the recording is of the highest quality possible. Sound operators must work closely with other people, such as producers, journalists and people being interviewed. They need patience and good communication skills. Working hours can be long and irregular and often include weekend work.

RANGE OF WORK:

- discuss the types of recordings required
- set up equipment for recording sessions
- mix sounds and use sound effects
- **edit** recordings

EDUCATION AND TRAINING

Sound operators need to know how to operate recording equipment and have a solid knowledge of digital recording and editing tools. Although some employers give on-the-job training, there are TAFE courses in sound production and university degrees in applied sciences that offer wider opportunities.

RADIO PRESENTER

JOB DESCRIPTION

The radio presenter is the person whose voice you hear presenting a program on the radio. Every radio show is different, and each presenter will have their own approach to broadcasting. Good communication skills and a clear, confident speaking voice are essential. They must also be able to think quickly and clearly under pressure.

RANGE OF WORK:

- read newspapers and press releases
- interview guests on air
- research and prepare stories for programs
- write scripts
- read news bulletins
- read advertisements
- comment on current affairs
- speak to talkback callers
- be familiar with online news sources

EDUCATION AND TRAINING

While there are no specific educational requirements for this job, it helps to have qualifications or experience in journalism, media or broadcasting.

BROADCAST TECHNICIAN

JOB DESCRIPTION

Many radio programs are live to air. It is the broadcast technicians who make sure that the studio equipment is in good working order at all times. Broadcast technicians install, maintain and repair radio broadcasting equipment. They need to be careful, methodical and aware of safety issues. They also need to work well under pressure.

RANGE OF WORK:

- advise on appropriate broadcasting equipment
- order and install new parts and equipment
- train people to use equipment correctly
- test and maintain equipment
- repair faulty equipment
- organise and set up equipment when broadcasting from an outside location

TIP

A radio presenter's job is very full-on. Each morning you need to find out what has been happening overnight – locally, nationally and internationally. Then, along with your production team, you decide which stories to cover. Once you're on air you will interview guests, take talkback calls and cover any important news that comes up while the program is running.

'A radio presenter's job is very full-on.'

WORDS IN PRINT AND DIGITAL MEDIA

Newspapers and magazines usually have both an online and a print edition. Each publication relies on a broad range of workers with very different skillsets and interests. Jobs include journalism, editing, photography, illustration, web design, marketing, video editing, blog writing and creation of social media content.

EDITOR-IN-CHIEF

JOB DESCRIPTION

A magazine or a newspaper will usually have an editor responsible for the content of each part of the publication, as well as an editor-in-chief who takes responsibility for the whole publication. An editor-in-chief needs good organisational and administrative skills, good communication skills and a strong understanding of what the readers of their publication want to read.

RANGE OF WORK:

- determine which stories to cover
- decide which journalist will cover each story
- set deadlines and make sure they are kept
- choose which stories and photographs to include
- manage a **budget**
- hire, train and manage staff

EDUCATION AND TRAINING

Qualifications include TAFE certificates in professional writing and editing, or a university degree in professional writing, journalism, communications or media studies. Business management qualifications are also very useful as this role has a strong focus on managing people and finances.

• JOURNALIST

JOB DESCRIPTION

Print journalists write articles and news reports for magazines and newspapers. They must have good research, writing and computer skills. They must also be able to write for a particular audience and produce a high standard of work, often to very tight deadlines. Newspaper journalists can choose to specialise in a variety of areas, including general news, international news, sport and travel.

RANGE OF WORK:

- research stories
- interview people and make notes
- write stories, articles, **features** or **columns**
- edit their work

EDUCATION AND TRAINING

Journalists can be employed by a newspaper or magazine or they can work freelance. Freelance writers don't need any qualifications to submit their work to newspapers or magazines, but professional journalists usually have tertiary qualifications. These qualifications are often in journalism, professional writing or editing. Some newspapers offer cadetships that are designed to provide on-the-job training.

• SUB-EDITOR

JOB DESCRIPTION

Sub-editors prepare articles and news reports for publication after journalists have written them. Sub-editors need good written communication skills and good computer skills. They must be able to work quickly under pressure and understand what the readers want. Sub-editors may work long and irregular hours, as they are ruled by their publication's deadlines. For example, a sub-editor at a major daily newspaper might work early mornings, evenings or weekends.

RANGE OF WORK:

- work with the editor-in-chief to decide on which stories should be included
- check spelling and grammar
- rewrite articles and stories where necessary
- edit articles and stories to the right length to fit into the space available in the publication
- write headlines for articles and captions for photographs

EDUCATION AND TRAINING

Employers look for TAFE certificates in professional writing and editing, and previous experience in journalism, editing and writing. Depending on the publication, competition for these roles can be fierce and it helps to have a university degree in professional writing, journalism, communications or media studies.

COLOUR IN PRINT AND DIGITAL MEDIA

Print and digital media is not just about words. It also relies heavily on pictures. Photographers, illustrators and graphic artists are just some of the people who work in this area. There are also jobs in printing, distribution and sales.

PRINTING MACHINE OPERATORS

JOB DESCRIPTION

Each night, printing presses all over Australia print newspapers and magazines so that they are ready for delivery to homes and shops each morning. A modern printing press works quickly, and turns out thousands of copies of a publication each hour.

EDUCATION AND TRAINING

Printing machine operators often start out as assistants to experienced printers, learning on-the-job. There are also TAFE courses in printing.

PHOTOGRAPHER

JOB DESCRIPTION

Photographers work with journalists, writers, editors and brand experts to take pictures of people, places and events.

RANGE OF WORK:

- discuss the type of photographs that might support a particular story
- decide which equipment to use to best suit different photo shoots
- arrange the camera, lighting and setting
- direct models and other people to compose interesting scenes
- use digital editing software to perfect colours or remove distracting elements from the finished image

EDUCATION AND TRAINING

Many TAFE colleges and universities offer courses in photography. People who are interested in photography need to get as much experience as possible and start building up a portfolio of photographs.

ILLUSTRATOR

JOB DESCRIPTION

Illustrators create illustrations for magazines, newspapers and books. Digital illustrators can work in multimedia and game design. They must be good at communicating with editors and clients. Many artists work as freelance illustrators.

RANGE OF WORK:

- talk with the client to find out what sort of artwork he or she wants
- negotiate payment for the job
- make sample drawings for the client to consider
- work with the client when making any changes in line with the client's preferences
- complete the artwork, often using digital art technologies.

EDUCATION AND TRAINING

People don't need specific qualifications to become an illustrator, however most illustrators have completed a diploma or degree in art or design. It is also important that illustrators build up a folio of work to show potential clients.

FILM AND TELEVISION

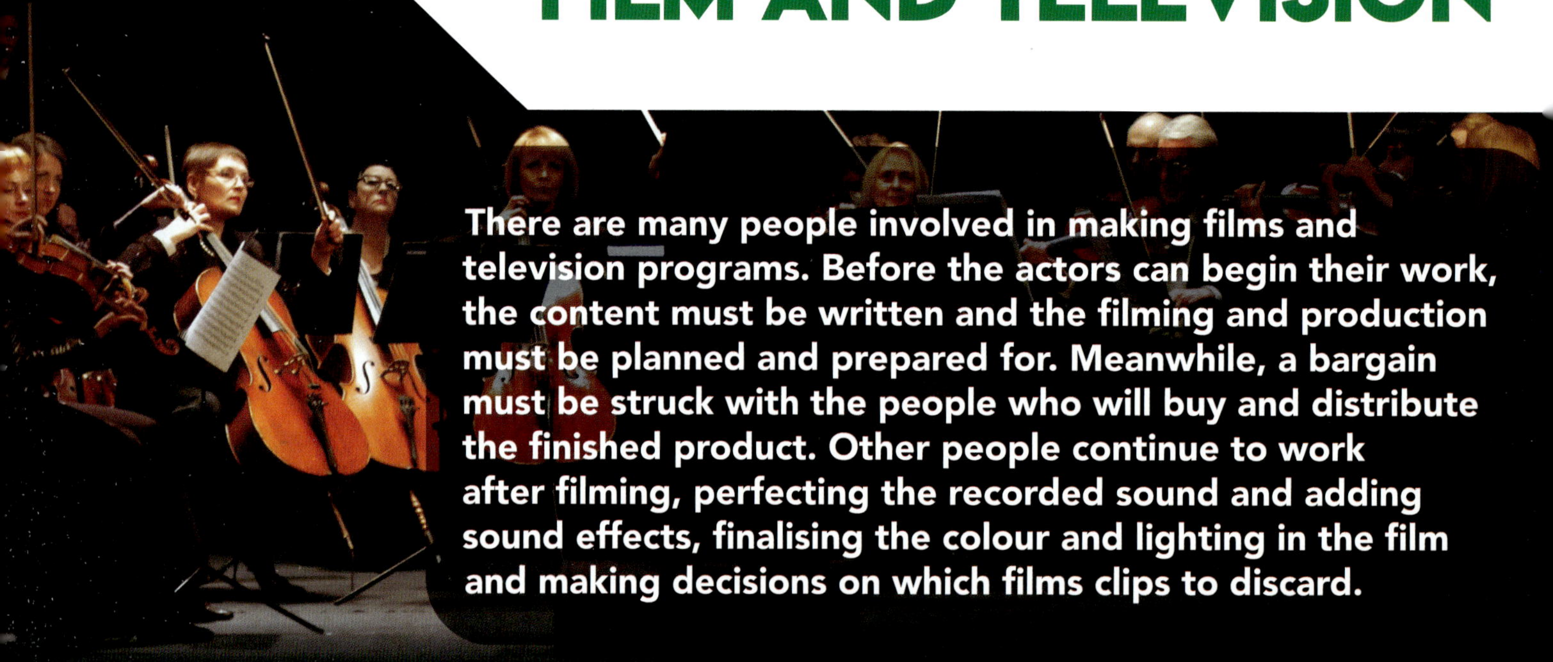

There are many people involved in making films and television programs. Before the actors can begin their work, the content must be written and the filming and production must be planned and prepared for. Meanwhile, a bargain must be struck with the people who will buy and distribute the finished product. Other people continue to work after filming, perfecting the recorded sound and adding sound effects, finalising the colour and lighting in the film and making decisions on which films clips to discard.

• DIRECTOR

JOB DESCRIPTION

Directors are in charge of actors and production crews on the set. They are the ones who must take ultimate responsibility for the finished film or television show. Directors need to understand and manage people. They must also be good decision makers and work well under pressure.

RANGE OF WORK:

- work with a producer to choose actors, film crews and other staff
- plan how a production will be shot
- decide on settings for a production
- direct actors in their performances
- direct the filming crew
- work with the editor to edit the film

EDUCATION AND TRAINING

To become a director you will need to have a lot of experience in film or television production. TAFE colleges and universities run courses in film, television and video production. A university degree in screen and media, film and television, theatre or creative arts will provide qualifications, opportunities for work experience and industry contacts.

KEY JOBS IN FILM AND TELEVISION

- Casting directors work closely with the director t choose the right actor for each role
- Editors put film and video **footage** together to create the final cut
- Directors of photography control and monitor the quality of the images on film
- Chief animators head a team of people who create drawings, models and computer-generated images for an animated production
- Costume designers design the clothes that the actors wear
- Composers and musical directors compose or choose the music to be used in a production

FILM PRODUCER

JOB DESCRIPTION

Television or film producers oversee the making of a film or television program. They need to be able to communicate well with people. They need planning and organisational skills, must be creative and have good business sense.

RANGE OF WORK:

- find stories, scripts or ideas
- raise money to finance productions
- work out the budget for productions
- find directors for productions
- work with directors to select staff and actors
- oversee entire productions

EDUCATION AND TRAINING

Producers need as much experience in the film and television industry as they can get. Many producers have TAFE and university qualifications in film and television or a degree in film, acting, journalism or communication.

ART DIRECTOR (FILM)

JOB DESCRIPTION

An art director creates the 'look' of the film or television program. This can mean anything from building a scene that looks like a street to one that resembles the inside of a space ship. It is important for an art director to be visually creative and to be able to communicate well with other people.

RANGE OF WORK:

- work with the director to agree on the overall look and feel of the production
- work with set designers, costume designers, special effects artists and production designers to decide upon set designs, colour schemes, lighting themes, and costumes
- oversee construction crews as they build sets
- direct the props buyer in decisions that help make sets look realistic

EDUCATION AND TRAINING

Although some people work as art directors without any specific qualifications, you need to have progressed through other roles within an art department to gain the necessary skills, knowledge and experience. A degree in film, television or theatre production may be useful, or there are TAFE courses in film and theatre, set design and art direction.

TIP

My work involves making corporate films and videos. I come up with concepts and ideas for our clients and I'm in charge of making those ideas come alive on film or video. I learned on-the-job while I was working in the film industry. You have to listen to other people's ideas while being true to your own.

Go to film school. There are so many fantastic courses available, and it's a really good way to make contact with people who work in the industry.

'Go to film school.'

ON-SET PRODUCTION STAFF

Each film or television production involves a large crew of people who work together on set. On-set production staff work in various areas, such as lighting, filming, hair and make-up and props. There are a number of jobs in each area.

KEY JOBS IN FILM AND TELEVISION PRODUCTION

- Animal handlers provide and care for animals on location
- Art department and props staff create the look and feel of a production by designing and dressing sets
- Catering staff provide food for the cast and crew on location
- Construction staff build the sets
- **Continuity** managers make sure images and actions are consistent throughout filming
- Location managers find locations for filming
- Sound managers monitor and record the sound

LIGHTING OPERATOR

JOB DESCRIPTION

Lighting operators organise and control the lighting on a film set or in a television studio. Lighting operators need to be organised, patient and good at dealing with problems. Lighting operators can be **gaffers** or **best boys**. The gaffer is the hea of electrics and lighting and the best boy is the gaffer's main assistant.

RANGE OF WORK:

- read the script and discuss lighting with the othe production staff
- set up lighting scaffolding
- lay down leads and put up lights according to th gaffer's instructions
- make sure all equipment is removed and stored properly at the end of each day
- keep lights and equipment tidy and organised

EDUCATION AND TRAINING

Lighting operators must be qualified electricians. Many learn about film and television lighting while working on-the-job, but there are courses in cinematography available through TAFE colleges.

HAIR AND MAKE-UP ARTIST

JOB DESCRIPTION

Hair and make-up artists create hairstyles and apply make-up to actors before they go on **set** to be filmed. Make-up artists have to be creative and artistic, but they also need to be practical, punctual and reliable.

RANGE OF WORK:

- design hair and make-up to suit each character
- help the actor to 'become' their character
- work with the continuity person to make sure actors look the same from one scene to the next

EDUCATION AND TRAINING

There are no formal educational requirements for this job, but it is important to have some technical training as well as some experience in working on a production set. There are TAFE courses in hair and make-up for film and television as well as privately run courses.

CAMERA OPERATOR

JOB DESCRIPTION

Camera operators film the events or scenes for film and television. They need to work as part of a team and be patient for long periods of time.

RANGE OF WORK:

- discuss with the director how the scenes should be filmed
- select and set up the right equipment
- decide where the cameras should go
- consult with lighting operators
- follow the director's instructions

EDUCATION AND TRAINING

There are no formal educational requirements for working as a camera operator and many skills are taught on-the-job. However, you usually need strong technical skills and practical experience in order to apply. An academic route would involve completion of a qualification in media production, media technology or photography.

POST-PRODUCTION STAFF

After the film or television show has been filmed, work begins for the post-production staff. Post-production staff add music, sound and visual effects to filmed footage to create the final product.

POST-PRODUCTION SUPERVISOR

JOB DESCRIPTION

The **post-production** supervisor oversees the post-production processes that happen after the film has been shot.

RANGE OF WORK:

- organise where and when post-production work is done
- decide who should do the different jobs
- set up the editing rooms with the right equipment
- organise the film to be transferred to the editing media
- maintain all editing equipment

EDUCATION AND TRAINING

Some people work in this area without formal qualifications. However, more people are gaining qualifications and experience by completing a degree or diploma.

KEY JOBS IN POST-PRODUCTION

- Music editors work with composers and editors to create soundtracks for films and television.
- Visual special effects staff work on film and television images to create something that was not there before. They use special computer programs designed to create and adjust film or video images.
- Sound mixers work in a mixing studio, mixing the soundtracks. This involves working out where different sounds will fit into the film.

SOUND EDITOR

JOB DESCRIPTION

A sound editor works closely with the editor to finalise the sound of a film. This is a very demanding job and sound editors need to be comfortable spending long periods of time alone, concentrating only on sound.

RANGE OF WORK:

- search for different sound effects
- organise and apply sound effects
- if necessary, re-record and replace dialogue that was recorded on location
- maintain post-production sound equipment

EDUCATION AND TRAINING

There are no formal qualifications needed for this job but sound editors must understand the editing and sound recording processes and the computer equipment required. A film or media production course such as a university degree or diploma in audio engineering and sound production is a good place to start.

ASSISTANT EDITOR

JOB DESCRIPTION

Assistant editors support the editor. They need to understand the different ways in which pictures can be joined together to tell a story. Assistant editors often have to work quickly under pressure. Patience and flexibility are essential skills.

RANGE OF WORK:

- view film or video with other production staff
- decide which shots need to be kept or cut out
- edit segments of film to the right length
- join the segments to create the right sequence
- edit music and special effects

EDUCATION AND TRAINING

There are many different courses in film editing. Experience, enthusiasm, persistence and a strong portfolio of short works can help you break into this small and very popular part of the film industry.

TIP

Get a good grounding in all aspects of film making and editing by making your own short films or getting a support job on a film set. Doing some qualifications will mean meeting new friends and contacts in the industry that can lead to work experience opportunities.

'qualifications will mean meeting new friends and contacts in the industry'

SUPPORT STAFF IN FILM AND TELEVISION

People involved in making films and television shows are supported by a large number of office staff. These people are vital to the smooth running of the production process.

• PRODUCTION MANAGER

JOB DESCRIPTION

Production managers are responsible for the business side of film and television productions. They need to be able to manage a broad range of people and coordinate many things at once. Production managers must be very organised people, good communicators and able to work well under pressure.

RANGE OF WORK:

- assist with the budget
- organise the cast and crew
- book film crew, equipment and studios
- maintain communication between different areas of production
- organise travel and accommodation
- manage shooting location arrangements

EDUCATION AND TRAINING

Film and television production managers have usually had experience in different areas of production before they become managers. This helps them understand the problems that each area of production faces. It also helps to have experience or qualifications in business administration, management or accounting, or have completed a film production course.

• PUBLICIST

JOB DESCRIPTION

In order for a film or television show to be successful, the public needs to find out about it. People who work in publicity are responsible for raising the public's interest in a production by advertising and promoting it.

RANGE OF WORK:

- write **media releases**
- send out media releases to newspapers, magazines, and radio and television stations
- organise press, radio, online and screen advertising for the production
- organise events to **promote** the production

EDUCATION AND TRAINING

To work in publicity, people need a background in publicity and public relations, or a university degree in public relations, communications or journalism.

RECEPTIONIST

JOB DESCRIPTION

The receptionist is very important. The receptionist is the first person someone meets or speaks to when they contact an office, so they need to present themselves in a manner that reflects the company's vibe and values. The job involves greeting people and helping them with their enquiries. Receptionists must enjoy dealing with the public and be able to work independently. They need good organisational and communication skills.

RANGE OF WORK:

- greet people when they come into the office and answer general enquiries
- answer telephone enquiries
- provide information
- arrange appointments
- sort incoming mail and organise delivery of outgoing mail
- send and receive emails and faxes
- carry out clerical work, such as word processing and filing

EDUCATION AND TRAINING

People who want to work as receptionists should consider a course in business administration that includes using Microsoft Office programs such as Excel and Word. This will give them the skills they need to apply for receptionist jobs.

ACCOUNTS CLERK

JOB DESCRIPTION

An accounts clerk in a production company works out the amount of money that the company receives and spends.

RANGE OF WORK:

- receive and send out invoices
- answer queries about accounts
- keep financial records
- check and follow up accounts that have not been paid

EDUCATION AND TRAINING

There are a number of certificates, diplomas and degrees available in business accounting.

TIP

Accounts and administration for a production company can involve a variety of work. You may answer the phone and welcome visitors, or manage minor accounts queries. Sometimes you may need to organise flights and accommodation for crew and cast members.

'Accounts and administration for a production company can involve a variety of work'

MULTIMEDIA

MULTIMEDIA PRODUCER

JOB DESCRIPTION

A multimedia producer is responsible for the overall development of a multimedia project. It is a job that calls for strong communication skills, an understanding of a range of different computer technologies and a good understanding of editing that enhances the meaning of content. The ability to imagine and create a multimedia project draws on a wide variety of skills and requires a talent for being able to see the bigger picture.

RANGE OF WORK:

- decide on content for multimedia projects
- work with writers and editors
- write and edit text
- record film and edit video footage
- work with graphic designs

EDUCATION AND TRAINING

There are many different specialties within digital media that combine to create multimedia. These skillsets include web design, graphic design, illustration, 3D animation, game design and video recording and editing, Knowledge of each of these different technologies is essential and these skills can be learned through a range of courses. Consider starting with a diploma in information technology or a degree in multimedia.

The word multimedia describes the bringing together of video, graphics, animation, text, sound and sometimes live action. Multimedia is used in entertainment, education, business and advertising. Many websites and computer games use multimedia. As technologies continue to develop, the number and range of jobs continue to grow. Many people who work in multimedia have a range of skills that enables them to work with and combine different types of media.

MULTIMEDIA GRAPHIC DESIGNER

JOB DESCRIPTION

Multimedia graphic designers work on interactive projects such as websites and interactive exhibitions like those used in museums and galleries. They are responsible for the way graphics are used in projects.

RANGE OF WORK:

- talk to the employer or client about their vision
- develop an idea for the design
- use software to produce the design
- create graphics that will combine with video, text and games in a multimedia project

EDUCATION AND TRAINING

People come to this job from a range of backgrounds, but it is a good idea to have a diploma in graphic design or graphic media, or a degree in information technology.

TIP

As a graphic designer at a multimedia company, you can work on a range of interesting projects, including interactive exhibitions for museums. You need to be creative first, then the essential computer skills come later. Get as much experience in different areas as you can. I started in video editing and learned other skills as I went along.

WRITING FOR MULTIMEDIA

JOB DESCRIPTION

People writing for multimedia need to be able to adapt their style to suit the audience they are writing for. Writers for multimedia also need to be able to write in a non-linear way. This means breaking up the information and presenting it in differing arrangements.

RANGE OF WORK:

- write multimedia pages for magazines and newspapers
- write content for web pages
- write digital educational material
- write text for computer games
- write content for interactive exhibits

EDUCATION AND TRAINING

There are no specific qualifications needed to write for multimedia, but many writing courses at TAFE colleges and universities now include writing for multimedia as a subject.

'Get as much experience in different areas as you can.'

WEB AND GAME

Many websites use multimedia to present information. People involved in designing websites might also work in other areas such as designing computer games and interactive exhibitions.

• WEBSITE ADMINISTRATOR

JOB DESCRIPTION

Website administrators – also called webmasters, web architects and web developers – develop and maintain websites. Website administrators need to have strong computer and problem solving skills. They must also be good at communicating with people who don't necessarily have these skills.

RANGE OF WORK:

- talk to the website developer about content and structure
- set up web servers and websites
- install operating systems and software
- check the website content and performance
- deal with any problems that arise

EDUCATION AND TRAINING

There are a number of pathways available including university degrees in computer science, diplomas in web design and certificates in web-based technologies.

• WEBSITE DEVELOPER /DESIGNER

JOB DESCRIPTION

Website developers design, produce and maintain websites. They need to fully understand their clients needs and must have good listening skills. People working in this area need to be creative as well as practical.

RANGE OF WORK:

- talk to the client about their proposed website
- discuss ideas and designs with the client
- lay out the written and visual web content
- review the website with the client
- maintain and update the contents of the website

EDUCATION AND TRAINING

There are a number of pathways available including university degrees in computer science, diplomas in web design and certificates in web-based technologies.

GAME DESIGNER /DEVELOPER

JOB DESCRIPTION

Game designers come up with ideas for computer games. People who become game designers generally love playing computer games themselves. Game designers need to keep producing something new that will be popular, so they have to be imaginative, focused and knowledgeable about what people who play computer games will like.

RANGE OF WORK:

- design the worlds where the games might take place
- create the characters that live in this world
- prepare storyboards and game maps that show what happens in the game
- write the game in a way that will motivate the players to keep returning to the world
- create a prototype for the game so that it can be tested

EDUCATION AND TRAINING

There are different levels of qualifications available in digital and interactive gaming, computer game design, animation and digital media technologies. To be a successful game designer, it is important to have a good understanding of the gameplay experience, technical skills in programming and 2D and 3D modelling.

COMPUTER ANIMATOR

JOB DESCRIPTION

Computer animators create images that come to life in film, television and video. They need to be self-motivated and able to work as part of a team. Computer animators must be able to use digital illustration and animation suites well and be creative in the way that they visualise images.

RANGE OF WORK:

- discuss with clients or employers what type of animation is required
- design the animation
- draw still characters and backgrounds
- create a series of drawings of each of the different moving parts that are later animated to create the illusion of movement
- create and film models and puppets
- use animation software to manipulate and control digital illustrations

EDUCATION AND TRAINING

Working in computer animation requires specific skills. A university degree in animation and interactive media, visual communication design, graphic design or graphic art and design will provide a good start as a computer animator.

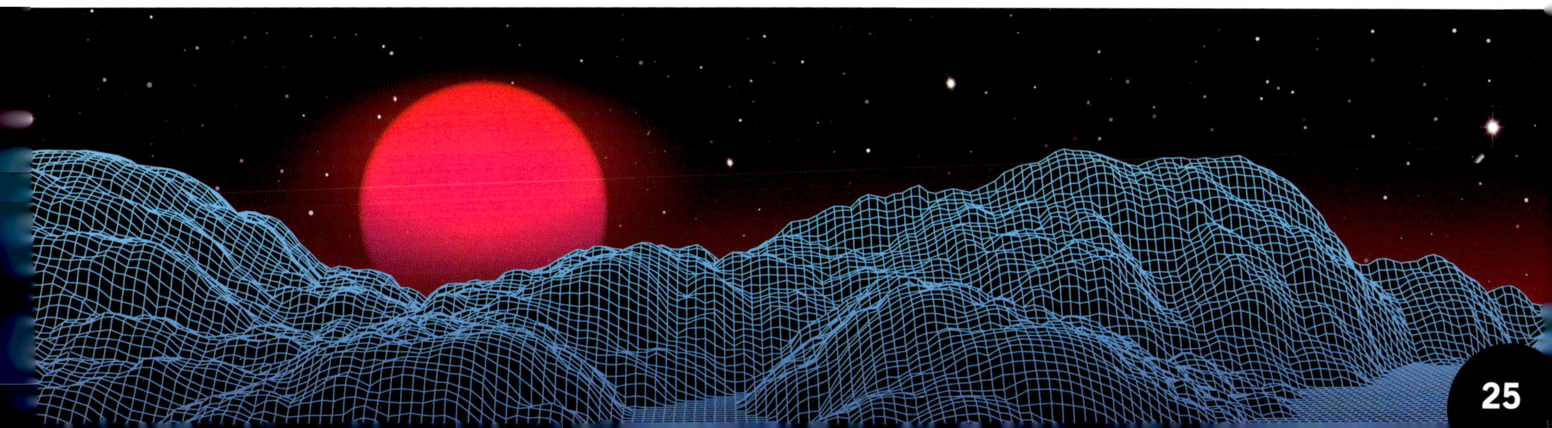

MEDIA ADVERTISING

ADVERTISING ACCOUNTS EXECUTIVE

JOB DESCRIPTION

Advertising accounts executives are involved in planning and managing advertising campaigns for clients, businesses and organisations. Their role is to plan and oversee advertising campaigns. They need to understand what their clients are looking for and be able to clearly explain their ideas to their clients. They must be creative and imaginative, but also organised and able to work well under pressure.

RANGE OF WORK:

- talk to the client to understand their product
- do research to find out as much as possible about the client and their service or product
- come up with ideas for an advertising campaign
- present these ideas in **draft** form to the client
- coordinate the campaign and oversee the work of different departments to make sure the campaign comes together
- keep the client involved in the process to make sure they are happy with the end results

EDUCATION AND TRAINING

Advertising account executives usually have a degree in advertising, communication or marketing and experience in advertising.

Advertising is all about influencing people to act in certain ways – usually to buy certain products or to use particular services. Advertisers often use the media to do this. As more new media forms are introduced, advertising methods continue to vary and the future job opportunities become more exciting and dynamic. Most people who work in advertising are employed by advertising agencies, but there are also opportunities for freelance work, or to work for companies in-house.

COPYWRITER

JOB DESCRIPTION

Copywriters write the words that are used in advertisements. They write for all sorts of media including magazines and newspapers, television, film and radio or brochures and newsletters. Digital copywriting involves developing written content for web pages and online promotions. Copywriters must have good communication skills, be creative and imaginative, have a very strong command of written language and have a good understanding of the way other people think.

RANGE OF WORK:

- discuss the product or service with the client
- research the reasons people buy this product or service
- work with the art director to develop ideas
- write text for the advertisement
- present a draft of the advertisement to the client
- discuss the advertisement with the people responsible for creating it in its final form

EDUCATION AND TRAINING

People from all sorts of educational backgrounds become copywriters. Most have some tertiary qualifications in arts, journalism, media studies, advertising or marketing.

MEDIA DIRECTOR

JOB DESCRIPTION

Media directors decide which medium to use for a particular advertisement. They are responsible for making sure an advertisement is seen, heard or read by as many people as possible. Media directors must understand the different forms of media and how they work. They must also have good business sense. Some media directors work by themselves while others work with a team of support staff including media planners and media buyers.

RANGE OF WORK:

- follow trends in entertainment
- decide which media will reach the most people
- work out which media will give value for money
- negotiate terms with the chosen media group

EDUCATION AND TRAINING

To become a media director it is common to have a university degree in communications or media and have a few years experience in different areas of the media.

'... get some work experience while you're still at university.'

TIP

Working in advertising is exciting, and very competitive. Try and get some work experience while you're still at university to help you find a job in the field once you finish study. Work on presentation and speaking skills. It is important for advertising executives to be able to present ideas for an advertising campaign.

OTHER JOBS IN MEDIA

There are many other important jobs in advertising that involve the production of advertisements. What people actually do to create the advertisement will depend on what kind of advertisement is being created and where it is to be shown.

• ART DIRECTOR (MEDIA)

JOB DESCRIPTION

Art directors work with copywriters to form a creative team. They translate the copywriter's ideas into pictures and graphics. Art directors work alone or with copywriters to develop the visual side of an advertising campaign. They need to have strong visual communication skills and be very confident in their approach. Art directors must be both creative and business-like to do their job effectively.

RANGE OF WORK:

- understand and keep up-to-date with what is popular in advertising
- talk to clients about what they want to achieve with their advertisement
- come up with ideas and develop the visual side of the advertisement
- meet with clients for feedback on the ideas
- work with copywriters to create the written content

EDUCATION AND TRAINING

Most art directors have a degree in media and communications or a diploma in graphic arts.

DESKTOP PUBLISHER

JOB DESCRIPTION

Desktop publishers arrange images on a page or screen in a way that best presents the content to its audience. Their job is to bring the idea designed by the copywriter and art director into reality. Desktop publishers need to have good communication skills and strong technical skills. They must also be creative in their approach to a project and aware of the latest digital techniques.

RANGE OF WORK:

- select images to use in a project
- make sure images and photographs are of the right standard for the intended media
- use computer software to create different effects
- arrange words and images in the most effective way

EDUCATION AND TRAINING

Qualifications in graphic design or multimedia would be useful for working in this area.

TIP

I started my working life as a print finishing artist in a family printing business and worked my way up to become a graphic designer. Then I got a different job as a designer in an advertising agency where I progressed to the position of art director.

Most of my training has been on-the-job, which is unusual now because most people in my position have some kind of university degree. I work in a very energetic, creative environment and the flexibility appeals to me. I know what I've got to do and when I have to do it by, but how I do it is up to me. The only things I don't like are short deadlines and trying to make decisions that need to make lots of different people happy.

A few words of advice:
Get a degree specialising in advertising and stick to your goals.

MANNY MOORE
ART DIRECTOR

'Get a degree'

GET FUTURE READY

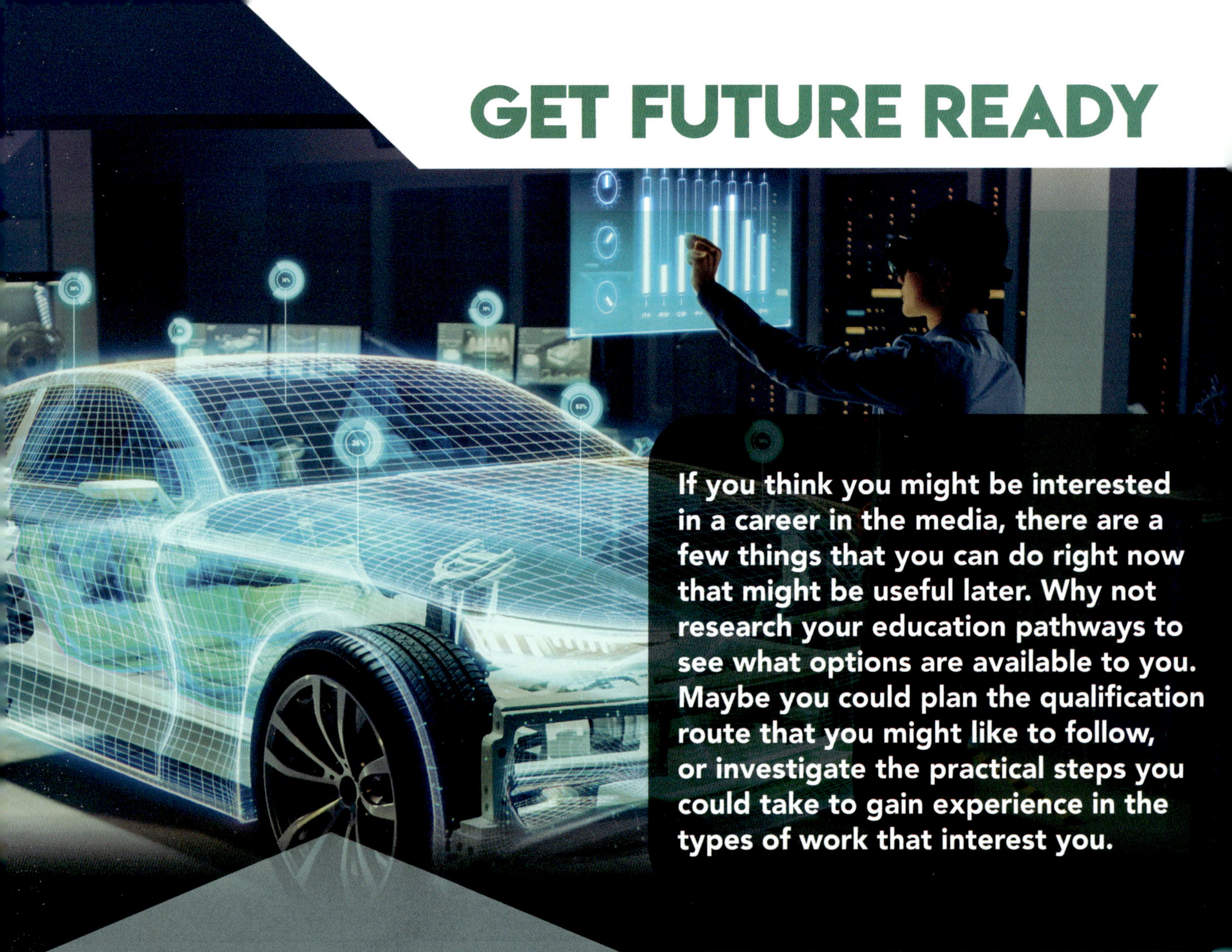

If you think you might be interested in a career in the media, there are a few things that you can do right now that might be useful later. Why not research your education pathways to see what options are available to you. Maybe you could plan the qualification route that you might like to follow, or investigate the practical steps you could take to gain experience in the types of work that interest you.

THE FUTURE

PRACTICAL EXPERIENCE

- work on a school newspaper or magazine
- help produce a school play
- make costumes and do make-up for school plays
- if your school doesn't already have one, see if you can start up a school radio station
- make videos by yourself or with friends and learn how to edit them
- talk to people who work in the media you're interested in
- find work experience on weekends or holidays in different areas of the media – some communities will have a radio station, magazine, newspaper or television station that needs volunteers
- write a blog or create content for your own YouTube channel

DO YOU NEED QUALIFICATIONS?

Media skills are becoming increasingly relevant to many areas of work – not just the media industry. There are courses at universities and TAFE colleges that specialise in the large range of media jobs available today and into the future. High schools now offer digital graphics and animation, web, app and game design, and video creation and editing. If you are interested in being in front of the camera or microphone, drama or music courses are a must. Writers and editors are essential to the media industry and those skills are taught in communications courses that include journalism, creative writing and screenwriting. Sound and lighting is a specialised area of study. Actors and presenters need costumes made by fashion design graduates. Hair and make-up artistry are taught in TAFEs, as is set design. Filming locations are found and documented by trained photographers and videographers.

GLOSSARY

advertising campaign organised series of advertisements to promote a product or service

best boy assistant to the chief electrician on a television or film crew

budget estimate of how much money is available and how much will be spent on a project

column regular section of a newspaper on a particular subject or written by a particular journalist

continuity consistency and agreement of details in different sessions of filming

draft first version of a piece of writing or drawing

edit refine a piece of written work for publication or finalise film footage for distribution

feature distinctive or regular newspaper article that tackles a subject in an in-depth way

footage film that has been shot for a television program or a movie

freelance self-employed person offering services for a set amount of time or single project

gaffer chief electrician on a television or film crew

internship opportunity for undergraduate students to gain unpaid or low-paid work experience

live television, radio or Internet broadcasts that are transmitted while being filmed or recorded

media release item of information sent to the media to inform, advertise or promote an event

post-production finishing video and audio in a film or television production before public release

promote publicise and sell a product, service or event

set setting for a play or a film, usually in a studio

INDEX